101 MANDALAS FOR RELAXATION

Benmore Book   Vol.8

101 Mandalas For Relaxation:

Big Mandala Coloring Book for Adults 101 Images Stress Management Coloring Book For Relaxation, Meditation, Happiness and Relief & Art Color Therapy(Volume 8)
by Benmore Book

Copyright: Published in the United States by Benmore Book

Published September 2019

All rights reserved. No part of this publication may be reproduced, stored in retrieval system, copied in any form or by any means, electronic, mechanical, photocopying, recording or otherwise transmitted without written permission from the publisher. Please do not participate in or encourage piracy of this material in any way. You must not circulate this book in any format. Benmore Book. does not control or direct users' actions and is not responsible for the information or content shared, harm and/or actions of the book readers.

ISBN: 9781690164616

This book belongs to

Thank You

Made in the USA
Monee, IL
14 January 2020